Worship from the Heart

How to connect your heart with the heart of Jesus

Veronica Bean

WESTBOW
PRESS®
A DIVISION OF THOMAS NELSON
& ZONDERVAN

WestBow Press books may be ordered through booksellers or by contacting:

WestBow Press
A Division of Thomas Nelson & Zondervan
1663 Liberty Drive
Bloomington, IN 47403
www.westbowpress.com
1 (866) 928-1240

ISBN: 978-1-5127-4236-7 (sc)
ISBN: 978-1-5127-4237-4 (hc)
ISBN: 978-1-5127-4235-0 (e)

Library of Congress Control Number: 2016908527

Print information available on the last page.

WestBow Press rev. date: 05/19/2016

Contents

Introduction

There is purpose for the worship service. It's no longer just the time we greet our friends and sing a few songs before the preacher comes up to speak. This is the time we connect with the Lord, receive from Him, and get direction for our lives.

As a child, I went to church regularly and had fun singing the hymns and worship songs. I would listen to the other people around me and watch the choir and worship team on stage. But honestly, I never experienced true worship during those years—the kind of worship where I enjoyed deep fellowship with the Lord. Then one day as a teenager, I found a church where the people loved to praise and worship God. It was a church full of "Jesus-lovers," and they were so enthusiastic in their expression. Instead of just singing songs, I learned that I could direct my songs to God Himself and open my heart to Him. When everyone would sing to the Lord with all their hearts, there was a very tangible sense of God's presence in the sanctuary. The more I opened my heart to God, the more He opened Himself to me, and my relationship with the Lord became real and personal.

That marked me forever. Later, if I found myself in a worship service that seemed stale, lifeless, and without His presence in manifestation, I would have such a craving for Jesus. I realized that I could never again be satisfied with the mere singing of songs.

That is what inspired this book. I believe it is possible for us to have the most wonderful encounters with the Lord *every time* we open our hearts to Him in worship. Times of worship, whether at home or at church, do not have to be boring and dry. We never have to come away from a moment of worship feeling disappointed, frustrated, or empty. We can connect with the living God *every time*!

Essentially, there is no wrong way to worship that I would need to tell you the right way. Everyone is unique in their expression. The only absolutely necessary element is the heart-to-heart connection with Jesus.

Jesus is indescribably amazing, fascinating, funny, smart, creative, and everything else you could ever imagine. It is deeply satisfying to be with Him. He never criticizes or accuses us. In fact, He uplifts us and encourages us more than anyone else could. Your spirit longs to be in close contact with Him; and the most unbelievable part is that He longs to be close to you.

As you read this book, understand that worship is not only for church time. Worship is a way of living—opening our heart to God in all the happy or dark places of life. Learning how to worship the Lord in private will set our course straight and bring us sanity of mind and heart. Also, learning how to worship in a group will bring great freedom to a church and powerfully advance the Kingdom of God.

If you have ever been in a worship service—watching individuals being touched by the Lord and longing for that same life-transforming touch from Jesus—then this is the book for you. And if you are the type of person who has had numerous encounters with the Lord, are addicted to His sweet love, and can never get enough—this book is also for you.

It is really true that we get out of the worship service what we put into it, so let's learn to put our whole heart into blessing, celebrating, admiring, and loving Jesus. Then get ready to experience some of your greatest moments with the Lord.

Veronica Bean

Chapter 1

Heart

It's a heart thing.

Christianity, being saved, living for God, worship, or whatever you want to call it—is a heart thing.

Humans are spirit beings possessing a soul and living in a body.

> Now may the God of peace Himself sanctify you completely; and may your whole *spirit, soul, and body* be preserved blameless at the coming of our Lord Jesus Christ. (1 Thessalonians 5:23 NKJV; emphasis added)

With the body, we are able to contact things in this natural world. We eat, pick up objects, drive a car, and so on. Our soul deals with the intellectual realm and has three functions: our mental abilities, our willpower, and our emotions. This is how we think, reason, learn, and express feelings. But with our spirit, which is the heart of us, we contact the spiritual world where God is.

John 4:24 says, "God is a Spirit."

So, God is not a mind, He is a Spirit. We can only connect with God through our own human spirit, not with our minds. It is a spirit-to-spirit, or heart-to-heart, connection. Sure, our mind is involved and helps us to focus on the Lord; yet too many times our mind can be a hindrance to truly connecting with Him.

Real worship is not a mental, logical thing. We don't reach God by thinking it all through or figuring Him out. We don't need to learn protocol, ceremonial traditions, or liturgy to approach God. True worship is deep admiration that opens a heart-to-heart connection with the Lord. It all begins to make sense when your heart opens up and connects with Jesus' heart.

True Worshipers

A true worshiper is someone who has fallen hopelessly in love with Jesus, and whose heart pitter-patters for Him. They see Jesus everywhere and are enraptured and enthralled with Him. This is a far cry from empty ceremony and religious duty.

Here is how Jesus describes true worshipers:

> But the time is coming—indeed it's here now—when true worshipers will worship the Father *in spirit and in truth*. The Father is looking for those who will worship Him that way. For God is Spirit, so those who worship Him must worship *in spirit and in truth*. (John 4:23—24 NLT; emphasis added)

Notice, He is not looking for "worship" per se, but He is looking for "worshipers." And He is looking for a very specific kind of worshiper—one who worships Him *in spirit and in truth.*

Jesus mentions "true worshipers," which, by the very words, implies that there can also be worship that may not be true. Jesus defined true worship with these two remarkable words: "in *spirit* and in *truth.*" Worship in spirit is worship that comes straight from your heart. Worship in truth is worship that is honest and sincere.

Let's consider the first part: "in spirit." Worship is a spiritual, or heart-involved, activity.

True love and admiration comes from deep within, from the bottom of your heart, from the depth of your gut, and it radiates out of every part of your being.

Remember when you first fell in love and your whole being was consumed with thoughts of your lover? A huge smile was indelibly etched upon your face, and sweet words flowed out of your mouth for your lover.

Time doesn't diminish true love. The giddiness might subside, yet after years of marriage the love is still there—and actually deepens as you learn to take care of each other. But, simply put, true love comes out of your heart and is evident on the outside.

If I were to go to the card shop to buy a card for my husband, I would browse through dozens of cards to find that one card that expressed exactly what I would really like to say to my sweetheart.

But if I just grabbed any card as I ran past and handed it to my husband, without putting any thought or heart into it, he would know it and would feel the lack of heart. The best card would be one that perfectly expresses my heart to my lover; and he would be touched when he reads it.

Worship is simply loving God; and it must be honest and wholehearted in order to touch His heart.

It's easy to tell when you are truly sincere with your love and when you are not. It grabs God's attention when you truly love Him. He knows the ones who really love Him.

> But if anyone loves God, this one is known
> by Him. (1 Corinthians 8:3 NKJV)

God can tell when our hearts are sincere or when we are only trying to impress Him (or others around us). As soon as we begin to speak to Him from our hearts, we have His attention. And wow! What He will do for someone who truly loves Him! He will literally move heaven and earth for those who love and trust Him.

> For the eyes of the LORD run to and fro
> throughout the whole earth, to shew himself
> strong in the behalf of them whose heart is perfect
> toward him. (2 Chronicles 16:9a KJV)

If your heart is perfect (that is, complete or whole-hearted) toward the Lord, He will show Himself strong on your behalf. He will reveal His strength and do miracles for you. You don't have to be perfect, but your heart and worship must be perfect and whole-hearted.

Put Your Whole Heart into It

The greatest precept in the Bible is to worship or love "the Lord thy God with all thy heart, and with all thy soul, and with all thy strength, and with all thy mind" (Luke 10:27 KJV). Do you really love Jesus? How could you express your love for Him? You demonstrate your love when you put your whole heart, your entire mental focus, and even your emotions and body language into your worship.

> And whatever you do, do it *heartily*, as to the Lord and not to men. (Colossians 3:23 NKJV; emphasis added)

Worship heartily. Put your whole heart into it. Love Him with *all* your heart.

> Sing, O daughter of Zion! Shout, O Israel! Be glad and rejoice *with all your heart*, O daughter of Jerusalem! (Zephaniah 3:14 NKJV; emphasis added)

Put your whole heart into it. Do you have any passion in you? When you sing a song to the Lord, do you truly mean every word of it? You could let the song dribble out of your mouth with no consideration of what you're actually saying, or you could mean every single word from the bottom of your heart. True worship is when we worship Him whole-heartedly. These are the kind of worshipers God is looking for and the ones on behalf of whom He shows Himself strong.

True Worship Begins in Your Heart

True worship that God desires comes from your heart. It begins in your heart and then is expressed through your mind and body. What is happening down in your heart during worship is much more important than what your hands, mouth, and body are doing. The body language is just the expression of what is in your heart.

Think about where your heart is the next time you're praying or singing to the Lord.

Jesus said of the religious leaders,

> These people draw near to me with their mouth,
> and honor me with their lips, but their heart is far
> from me (Matthew 15:8 NKJV).

Their heart was far from Him, even though it looked like their mouth was saying or singing the right words. There's a big difference between singing a song of worship and worshipping. Worshipping is pouring out your heart to the Lord, connecting heart-to-heart.

I remember one experience I had in a prayer meeting. We would usually start out with worship before flowing over into prayer for the church. I had my hands raised and I was singing, but my mind was somewhere else. I looked up and realized my hands were in the air, and I thought, *Oh yeah, I'm supposed to be worshipping!* Then, I began to put my heart into it.

> Let us lift up our heart with our hands unto God
> in the heavens. (Lamentations 3:41 KJV)

Lift up your heart along with your hands. When your hands go up to bless the Lord, your heart should be right there, too.

God is not looking for someone who can sing magnificently or play an instrument masterfully. He does like excellence and skill, but He prefers your heart above all. I really love playing the piano, but sometimes I have found my playing to be a distraction to my being able to connect with the Lord. Whenever I focus on the chords and try to make my singing and playing beautiful, I find that I am not focusing on Jesus as much. And whenever I focus on Jesus, I couldn't care less how my music sounds because I am so absorbed in Him. This is a great truth: Jesus is impressed with your heart of love for Him, not with your fancy music. This is not to say that we shouldn't improve our musical abilities, but "man looks on the outward appearance, the Lord looks at the heart" (1 Samuel 16:7).

Engage Your Heart

Singing songs to the Lord without putting your heart into it would be comparable to riding a lawnmower without engaging the blade. You might look like you're mowing as you ride around the yard but no grass is being cut.

Imagine yourself during a time of worship. Maybe you're just going through the motions. You might be singing along with the others; but you are looking around, watching the other worshipers, and thinking about anything and everything. You are there but you are disengaged.

Then you decide to engage your heart—you begin to really mean the words you're singing and you sing them with all of your heart to the Lord. It's just like a lawnmower that engages the blades and makes a smooth path through the overgrown grass. As soon as you engage your heart, the relationship begins to flow between you and Jesus.

Singing a worship song is not the same as worshipping. Listening to worship music is not the same as worshipping.

> As for you, son of man, the children of your people are talking about you beside the walls and in the doors of the houses; and they speak to one another, everyone saying to his brother, "Please come and hear what the word is that comes from the LORD."
>
> So they come to you as people do, they sit before you as My people, and they hear your words, but they do not do them; for with their mouth they show much love, but their hearts pursue their own gain.
>
> Indeed you are to them as a very lovely song of one who has a pleasant voice and can play well on an

instrument; for they hear your words, but they do
not do them. (Ezekiel 33:30—32 NKJV)

Did you know that it's possible to be distracted both negatively
and positively from deep worship? There might be people talking
or a baby fussing nearby that attracts your attention and distracts
you from worship. But it is possible to also be distracted by the
amazing instrumentalists or singers with "a very lovely song", and
a "pleasant voice." When you block out everyone around you and
worship the Lord from your own heart, then your heart is engaged
in worship and the relationship flows.

Personalize it

I heard a well-known worship leader, Nancy Harmon, say
something that impressed me, "You haven't begun to worship
until you use your own words."

If you are having a struggle engaging your heart, try interjecting
your own words. I have found that I connect immediately with
the Lord when I start talking to Him from my own heart.

As long as you merely use someone else's words or lyrics, your
heart cannot fully engage with the Lord. But even if you only say
two or three words that are straight from your heart, those few
words will engage your heart and initiate an intimate conversation
with Jesus.

Avoid using cliché words or worn-out phrases. Try to use
descriptive words that truly express your heart to God.

That makes me think about the card I gave to my husband. Even after I have found the perfect card that says what my heart feels, often I will hand-write something at the bottom of the card. Those few words I hand-write on the card before I sign my name are the most heartfelt and personal.

Using your own words of worship makes it much more personal. And if you often speak to God from your heart, you will develop a very close, ongoing relationship with Him. If you open your heart and let Him know everything about you, He will also open His heart to you and reveal Himself completely.

> Draw near to God and He will draw near to you.
> (James 4:8 NKJV)

As you worship *in spirit*, with all your heart, you are drawing close to God. The Bible says that if you do, He will in turn draw close to you. When He comes close, you begin to experience the tremendous love He has for you. You begin to see clearly and understand things that had previously been very confusing. When He draws near to you, He imparts His superior wisdom and even the intricate secrets of God.

> He reveals deep and secret things. (Daniel 2:22a
> NKJV)

> Truly your God is the God of gods, the Lord
> of kings, and a revealer of secrets. (Daniel 2:47
> NKJV)

The person who has My commands and keeps
them is the one who [really] loves Me; and
whoever [really] loves Me will be loved by My
Father, and I [too] will love him and will show
(reveal, manifest) Myself to him. [*I will let Myself
be clearly seen by him and make Myself real to him.*]
(John 14:21 AMP; emphasis added)

What an amazing thing to know the Lord's secrets! How awesome
that God would let Himself be clearly seen and make Himself
real to me as I worship Him *in spirit*! I have had moments in
worship where the Lord danced with me, sang to me, hugged me,
or spoken very encouraging words to me. Those experiences with
Him are the greatest thrills of my life! They definitely beat going
to Disney World, having a new baby, eating chocolate ice cream,
and any other thing that thrills. My greatest joy in life is being in
His presence. My deepest satisfaction comes from spending time
with Jesus in the secret place.

You make known to me the path of life; you will
fill me with joy in your presence, with eternal
pleasures at your right hand. (Psalm 16:11 NIV)

Engaging our heart in worship is usually easier if we choose songs
that particularly touch our own heart. When we worship the
Lord, it is much more personal when we sing songs that are our
favorites, songs that mean something special to us.

One of my favorite songs to sing to the Lord has a line in it that
goes, "When I was lost and alone in the darkness, You found
me." Every time I sing it, my mind goes to the time I was in Bible

School, just barely making it on the limited income I had from waitressing. Just two years before, my parents had divorced, and my emotions were still very messed up. I had my face down on the carpet in the bedroom of my apartment, crying out to God, and feeling so afraid. It was a very dark time of my life; and I couldn't see how Jesus could take the mess I was and make something wonderful out of it. But Jesus reached down and found me! He brought me out of that difficult place. He has since blessed me so much that it is hard to believe I was ever in such a low place in my life. So every time I sing those words, my mind goes back to that moment; and I feel such gratefulness that tears come to my eyes.

There are other worship songs that don't really connect with my heart. I just can't relate to the lyrics because they don't express the things in my own personal heart. So then, find the songs that mean something to you and are easy for you to engage your heart.

It doesn't matter what is in someone else's heart. What is in your own heart for the Lord? This is what touches His heart: not you repeating everyone else's words, but you speaking from your own heart to Him.

It all comes down to this— no matter what song you're singing, what words you're saying, what your hands are doing, or what position you're holding; the thing that really counts is the involvement of your heart. Worship Him *in spirit.*

Chapter 2

Real

> But the time is coming--indeed it's here now--
> when true worshipers will worship the Father *in
> spirit and in truth*. The Father is looking for those
> who will worship Him that way. For God is Spirit,
> so those who worship Him must worship *in spirit
> and in truth*. (John 4:23—24 NLT; emphasis
> added)

The second ingredient of true worship, as Jesus defined it, is "in truth."

In order for us to be true worshipers and experience a close and personal relationship with Jesus, we must be absolutely and completely honest. Even a slight amount of pretense can be like a wall between us and the Lord. We must be real.

During a time of worship, if you feel disconnected or detached, or are feeling like you are not really connecting with the Lord, do not proceed any further.

To tell the truth, sometimes we think we are worshipping because the music is so emotionally stirring. There are some worship songs with rich, warm chords. When you combine that with a band of skilled musicians, it can really move you emotionally. The music itself can sometimes bring you to tears; yet, your heart can still be distant from God.

Be completely honest with yourself and admit when you are just going through the motions. Stop right there and open your heart to God in pure honesty. Sometimes, I have said to the Lord, "Ok Lord, I am not really connecting with you; I am just going through the motions and enjoying the music." And when I begin telling Him how I am truly feeling and what is bothering me, the relationship begins to flow. Simple honesty is the best opener of meaningful conversation.

I have an aunt who is extremely good with relationships. One day, I asked her what she thought was the most important element for building a relationship with someone. I was guessing that she might say, "spending time with them," or "giving a gift;" but her answer surprised me. She said in one quick simple word, "Honesty. You have to let people know what you like and don't like. Let them know if they offended you, and so forth. Be completely honest."

Being sincere is so paramount to a good relationship. The word "sincere" comes from a Greek root and is defined as—"examined in the sunlight and found pure." This gives the picture of holding something up to the light to see if it is cracked or has any defect. The word "sincere" also means—"pure, unmixed." There is no duplicity or hypocrisy. Being pure-hearted and truthful is what makes for a good relationship.

To be dishonest or deceptive in order to gain benefit from someone is what con artists do. To lie to someone is terrible. You would have to betray a person's trust in order to persuade them to believe your lie. The Lord will NEVER lie. The Bible says that it is, "impossible for God to lie" (Hebrews 6:18 KJV). If He ever told even just one lie, it would make you doubt everything He has ever said. So also, our credibility is marred if we are deceptive in any way.

We must be entirely open and sincere with ourselves and with God. It is funny how we try to hide things from the Lord, the One who knows everything about us.

> O LORD, You have examined my heart and know everything about me. You know when I sit down or stand up. You know my thoughts even when I'm far away. You see me when I travel and when I rest at home. You know everything I do. You know what I am going to say even before I say it, LORD. (Psalms 139:1—4 NLT)

He knows things about us that we don't even know about ourselves. He knows how we think and what captivates our thoughts; because He has studied human personalities from the beginning of time. He created us. So, if He already knows us and has not annihilated us but has shown love to us consistently, it is safe to go ahead and open up to Him.

> And Solomon, my son, learn to know the God of your ancestors intimately. Worship and serve Him with your whole heart and a willing mind. For the

LORD sees every heart and knows every plan and thought. (1 Chronicles 28:9a NLT)

Humility is Reality

When we speak of truthfulness, we are speaking of humility, for that is its clearest definition. Humility is simply "reality." To be humble is not to think of yourself too loftily, nor to think of yourself too lowly, but to see the truth about yourself.

My mother provided me with piano lessons when I was a child, and I was able to reach the advanced levels in my training. I have used the skills I developed for many years now, both in teaching piano and in playing for the church. To say that I cannot play the piano would not be humility but a lie. Yet, on the other hand, I am very aware that there are concert pianists who have travelled the world performing. They are far superior to me in their skills. So, to say that I am the greatest pianist ever would also be a lie. The truth is—I can play advanced levels of music but I still have far to go. Humility is reality.

Jesus died on the cross for us, to bring us into a sweet, fearless relationship with God. It is ONLY by the Blood of Jesus that we receive all the good things He provides. When we come to the Lord, we do not have to grovel, bemoan our weaknesses to Him, and try to give Him reasons to love us. Our sins have been washed away, so we now stand pure and right before Him.

Humility is reality. The reality is that Jesus has accepted us because of His own sufferings. Therefore, we can come confidently before Him and speak without any sense of intimidation, simply because of His great love. It is not pride and brashness but humility and reality that allow us to enjoy Him and to receive all the blessings of heaven.

Pride, on the other hand, is self-focused and causes us to believe lies about ourselves. For us to come barging in, articulating our accomplishments, and demanding our blessings is all empty and gets us nowhere with God. We are flat nothing apart from Him.

> Jesus also told this parable to people who were sure of their own goodness and despised everybody else. "Once there were two men who went up to the Temple to pray: one was a Pharisee, the other a tax collector. The Pharisee stood apart by himself and prayed, 'I thank you, God, that I am not greedy, dishonest, or an adulterer, like everybody else. I thank you that I am not like that tax collector over there. I fast two days a week, and I give you one tenth of all my income.' But the tax collector stood at a distance and would not even raise his face to heaven, but beat on his breast and said, 'God, have pity on me, a sinner!' I tell you," said Jesus, "the tax collector, and not the Pharisee, was in the right with God when he went home. For those who make themselves great will be humbled, and those who humble themselves will be made great." (Luke 18:9—14 GNB)

The Pharisee considered what he was doing "prayer," yet he never really connected with God because he was so artificial. Even if he was a decent person and had his life mostly together, he still had

17

some personal issues in which he needed God's help. Everyone does. The tax collector saw himself as he truly was. He worshipped *in truth*. Therefore, he was able to contact God. Humility draws you into God's favor. Just be real with Him.

> For God sets Himself against the proud (the insolent, the overbearing, the disdainful, the presumptuous, the boastful)--[and He opposes, frustrates, and defeats them], but gives grace (favor, blessing) to the humble. (1 Peter 5:5 AMP)

Another side of pride would be to come before the Lord like a beaten slave. Most people associate humility with lowliness like a slave, so how could this be considered pride? We have been united with Jesus. We are one with Him. It would be wrong for us to approach Him as a slave when His blood has already brought us near to Him. His Spirit has come into us and made us sons and daughters of God. It is reality, which is humility, to stand confidently before the Lord.

> But now you have been united with Christ Jesus. Once you were far away from God, but now you have been brought near to Him through the blood of Christ. (Ephesians 2:13 NLT)

There is a closeness that we now enjoy with the Lord that is very intimate. He is the "Lover of my soul."

There have been several times during intimate worship where I sensed the Lord telling me to put my shoulders back and pick up my chin. He is the, "lifter of my head" (Psalm 3:3 KJV).

Many people would see that cowering position as lowliness and humility, not as pride. But pride says, "I don't want to come by the way of the cross and the Blood of Jesus alone; I want to show God my dedication and effort. I want to do it my way. I can do this by myself. I am going to make Jesus so proud of me by my consecration." That is actually self-exaltation and egotism. The reality is—Jesus' blood is the only way to approach God—so just accept it His way.

> Therefore, brethren, *having boldness to enter the Holiest by the blood of Jesus*, by a new and living way which He consecrated for us, through the veil, that is, His flesh, and having a High Priest over the house of God, let us draw near with a *true heart* in *full assurance of faith*, having our hearts sprinkled from an evil conscience and our bodies washed with pure water. (Hebrews 10:19—22 NKJV; emphasis added)

When we come with a "true heart", we can have "boldness" and "full assurance of faith." Boldness and humility are two sides of the same coin. So, when we approach God, we come with the realization that we are accepted and righteous before Him because of the blood sacrifice of Jesus. Knowing this sure does take the pressure off. We do not have to put on a whole production for the Lord to notice us and to love us. What a relief!

There is no need to try to impress Him with my worship. I am who I am and God knows me completely. I am His child—born of God. An employee would need to try to impress the boss, but

I have a father/daughter relationship. I can be completely myself around Him.

Children do not have to act like they are grown up in order for their father to love them. Most fathers love the simple innocence of their children—mistakes and all. I do not have to act like I am more spiritually developed than I am. I am accepted and loved by God—mistakes and all. I can worship *in truth*.

Unleavened Bread

In regards to having sincerity and truthfulness in a good relationship, think about this:

In the Bible, there are many references to eating "unleavened" bread—especially at God's house or during His holy feasts. Jesus told us that leaven (or yeast) is symbolic of hypocrisy.

> Be on your guard against the *yeast* of the Pharisees, which is *hypocrisy*. (Luke 12:1 NIV; emphasis added)

Hypocrisy is phoniness or dishonesty. Just like yeast makes bread rise and be full of air, hypocrisy makes us full of hot air.

> Therefore let us keep the Festival, not with the old yeast, the yeast of malice and wickedness, but with bread *without yeast*, the bread of *sincerity and truth*. (1 Cor. 5:8 NIV; emphasis added)

When we partake of communion, we eat the unleavened bread and drink the grape juice or wine. The word "communion" is defined as—"fellowship, a sharing of intimate communication." We cannot have true communion—which is conversing together in deep levels of intimacy—with leavening in our bread. Therefore, we cannot have true fellowship or communion with any amount of fakery or hypocrisy. Insincerity blocks true fellowship. So if we get rid of pretense, we can enjoy rich communion with Jesus.

> Blessed are the *pure in heart*: for they shall see God. (Matthew 5:8 KJV; emphasis added)

The person who is sincere will find the favor of the Lord with them.

> Grace be with all them that love our Lord Jesus Christ *in sincerity*. Amen. (Ephesians 6:24 KJV; emphasis added)

> For we who worship by the Spirit of God are the ones who are truly circumcised. *We rely on what Christ Jesus has done for us. We put no confidence in human effort*, though I could have confidence in my own effort if anyone could. Indeed, if others have reason for confidence in their own efforts, I have even more! (Philippians 3:3—4 NLT; emphasis added)

I can understand how Paul felt. If anyone has reason for confidence in their own efforts, I sure do. I was born into a Christian home and went to church faithfully all my life. I have tithed since I received an allowance as a child. I graduated from Bible school and have served in the church for over 30 years. Surely, you would think all of that would earn me some special favoritism with the Lord. But I have to come to Jesus the same way that everyone must come— on the basis of His sacrifice on the cross. None of my human effort could bring me closer to God. It takes faith. Only when I come to the Lord in simple faith and reliance on His sacrifice do I feel His favor and tender kindness toward me.

There were some desperate times in my life that put me on my face before the Lord. The only thing I could pray was, "Lord, help me," as the tears poured out. He immediately came and knelt down over me. He rushed to my aid, comforted me tremendously, and poured out His love so gently.

> The LORD is near to those who have a broken
> heart, and saves such as have a contrite spirit.
> (Psalms 34:18 NKJV)

A contrite spirit is a sincerely remorseful heart. The Hebrew word for "contrite" means—"crushed, broken in pieces." When your life is broken and falling apart, and your heart is crushed, fall on your face before the Lord. He will be very near to you. He loves those cries for help from the carpet! Those desperate times have become my sweetest memories with Him.

Free from Self-Consciousness

Speaking of desperation, it seems that people who are in dire need of a touch from God do not care what other people think of them.

If they need the Lord desperately enough, they throw aside any sense of self-consciousness that would hold them back.

Self-awareness is one of the greatest hindrances to connecting with the Lord in deep worship. When you feel like people are watching you, or maybe overhearing you, it can be difficult to be completely open with the Lord. Often, we are worshipping in a group with other believers and not in private, so the feelings of self-consciousness can really hinder us from being real with God.

Think about going to a fitness center for the first time. You feel like everyone in the building is watching you and whispering about how unfit you are. Maybe you're afraid to make any grunts or groans because you know everyone would break out in laughter. If you fall off the treadmill or drop the weights on your foot, you wince and try your best to hold it in. You are consumed with self-consciousness when you first begin working out. But people who have been going to the gym for years have long ago overcome those thoughts. They proceed with their workout oblivious to everyone around them.

Stage fright is the same. I remember the first time I stood up in front of the class to audition for the lead role in a play. Being an extremely shy child, I was literally shaking all over. In fact, I overhead one child on the front row say to his friend beside him, "Her lips are shaking."

You have two choices—you can either quit going to the gym and quit trying out for parts, or just keep doing it in spite of the insecurities. Eventually, the stage fright leaves and you can walk right up on stage, grab the mic, and sing your heart out.

Going to church and worshipping together with other believers might feel very awkward for the first time. If you keep looking around, checking to be sure no one is staring at you, you will never be able to get completely real with the Lord and connect your heart to His. Knowing that other people are listening can definitely affect the quality of your worship.

Learn to get absorbed with Jesus and block out everyone else. The greatest thing that helps me overcome self-consciousness is closing my eyes. It is funny how we believe no one can see us when we can't see them. If you hang in there, you will eventually become oblivious to others around you and will be free to worship from your heart.

Remember the common phrase: "Dance like you do when no one is watching; sing like no one is listening"? The sense of self-consciousness will gradually diminish and you will be free to exercise your spirit at the spiritual gym in front of everyone. And, as I said earlier, if you are desperate to have a touch from God, you couldn't care less what people think of you.

Because our heart is unique, our worship will be expressed in unique ways. So there is no need in comparing our worship with those around us. John Wesley made a very helpful statement— "Let no one be bound by another's practice. But in every case, let due provision be made for intercourse with God." You do not have to worship like anyone else. Your worship does not have to look like your pastor's or your mother's worship. You can be the very unique person that you are, as long as you are making due provision for intercourse with God. Some would be horrified to think they had to be as dramatic in worship as those who are very expressive. And vice versa, the very expressive ones would be absolutely stymied if they had to worship quietly like others prefer to do. Be who you are; worship *in truth.*

Worship in Private

One of the best ways to prove that your worship is real and genuine is to worship the Lord in a place that is solitary. Find a place where no one is watching so that you can be free from trying to impress others. When it is just you and Jesus, your heart can be the most open and sincere.

Those who worship God only when other people are watching are seeking the approval of people. If you can honestly worship the Lord when no one is looking, then your worship is truly genuine and your heart is pure. Who you are in private is the real you.

Whatever you do in private is seen by God, and He will reward you openly before other people.

> But when you pray, go away by yourself, shut the door behind you, and pray to your Father in private. Then your Father, who sees everything, will reward you. (Matthew 6:6 NLT)

When you find satisfaction often in Jesus, the fruit of it will be evident to everyone.

Chapter 3

Aware

Have you ever been mumbling to yourself, lost in your thoughts, thinking that you were alone in a room, and then suddenly you became aware that someone else was there? Jesus is always with us and He sees and hears everything. But, since He is invisible, we often are unaware of Him.

Jesus told us,

> Lo, I am with you always, even to the end of the age. (Matthew 28:20b NKJV)

> For He Himself has said, "I will never leave you nor forsake you." (Hebrews 13:5 NKJV)

If the Bible says that He is always with us and will never leave us, then we can be sure that He is there when we don't even sense His presence. We have to just take this by faith. Even if we have absolutely no sensations confirming it, we still know that the Lord is with us because His Word says so.

Religious people have painted a picture of a God that is far away, the "Man upstairs" who is up in heaven somewhere. They portray God as the Creator that spun the world into existence and now sits back to watch things carry on.

On the contrary, the sacrifice of Jesus has brought us up close and personal with the Lord. We are one with God in complete, perfect union. No longer is He confined to a temple; we are His temple. He dwells with us and in us. His name is Emmanuel, which means, "God with us." He is very near to us; not far away and not hard to find.

> His purpose was for the nations to seek after God and perhaps feel their way toward Him and find Him—*though He is not far from any one of us.* (Acts 17:27 NLT; emphasis added)

One of God's seven redemptive names is Jehovah-Shammah, which means, "The Lord is there," or, "The Lord is present" (Ezekiel 48:35).

> I can never escape from Your Spirit! *I can never get away from Your presence!*
>
> If I go up to heaven, *You are there*; if I go down to the grave, *You are there.*
>
> If I ride the wings of the morning, if I dwell by the farthest oceans, *even there* Your hand will guide me, and Your strength will support me. (Psalms 139:7—10 NLT; emphasis added)

He is here! There is no place on the earth where He is not.

Here's the thing—if we really believe He is right here, just like the Bible says that He is, we will talk to Him differently. When we believe that the Lord is with us, we won't find it necessary to cry out for Him to come down. We don't need to sing for Jesus to come when He is already here.

If my husband was upstairs and I was downstairs, I would have to yell loudly for him to come to me. But if he was right there in the kitchen with me, I would talk to him in normal tones. I don't need to wonder if he hears me because I know that he loves me and has good ears. The same is true of God.

We don't need to cry out loudly for God, nor spend an hour begging the Lord to come. We never have to sing songs that ask the Holy Spirit to come down because He is omnipresent. Really, what we need to do is to become aware of His presence and to believe that He is right here. By faith, we can jump right into conversation with Him, knowing that He is very close and hears everything.

There are many times when my husband and I may be in the same room together, but are in separate worlds because we are doing different things. He may be reclined on the couch watching TV and I am sitting on the other couch playing games on my laptop. We may be oblivious to each other, but at any time I could turn my attention to him and engage in conversation. It is just that way with the Lord. Even though He is always with us, there are moments when we turn our attention to Him. As soon as we focus on Him, we become aware of Him.

As a younger Christian, I heard ministers preach on, "Practicing the presence of the Lord." What they meant was, practice your awareness of Him all throughout the day. While washing dishes, driving the car, at work, or at home, practice turning your thoughts toward Him. Talk to Him all the time about everything.

There was a lady shopping at a department store one day. When she saw a beautiful dress on one rack, she said to the Lord right out loud, "Oh, Jesus, what a beautiful dress!" There was a store clerk nearby. When he heard her say Jesus' name, he asked, "Is something wrong?" He assumed she was cursing like others have done, but she was simply in constant conversation with her best friend, Jesus.

Now, let's take this idea of awareness of God to the worship service. When the music cranks up, we are standing in our row and are expected to sing. Often, when we start out singing we are in another world, oblivious to God. Our mind may be distracted by our children fussing, the people in front of us talking, or the ushers walking past. It takes a lot of concentration to block out everything, become aware of the Lord, and direct our worship to Him.

Speaking to Him, Not Just of Him

One time at a wedding, as the minister was having the bride and groom repeat their vows to each other, he said to the groom, "Repeat this after me: Laura, I love you." The groom, with the expected amount of nervousness for such an occasion, parroted, "Laura, I love you." Then the minister said with a smile, "Now, look at Laura and say it." Everyone chuckled.

During worship, look at the Lord and say your words of praise *to Him*. It makes a huge difference in our ability to connect with the Lord. Imagine the difference between a person talking to himself or talking into the air, and a person actually talking to someone with that someone responding. It makes a big difference in your conversation when there is someone engaged in it with you. A dialogue is very different from a monologue. The Lord is really there, and you can have a face-to-face conversation every time. Talk to Him as if He were right there.

When I am aware that someone is right there beside me, I don't talk about them in third person. When my husband is standing in front of me, I wouldn't say things like, "My husband sure is great! He's so sweet and so good to me." He would definitely wonder who I was talking to. He would probably think, "Why are you talking about me as if I'm not here?"

The majority of worship songs are focused directly to the Lord, but there are some songs that use words like, "*He* is good, *He* is worthy," etc. There is no problem at all with singing songs in third person, but singing directly to the Lord is more conducive to deeper worship. Many times, I will just switch the words in the song from *He* to *You*, and suddenly I have a greater awareness of His presence.

Visualize Jesus

Your heart is not in what your mind is not on. This means that if your thoughts are not focused on the Lord, neither is your heart. So, as you begin to set your mind on the Lord and see Him with your spirit's eyes, your heart will connect with His.

Since the Bible says that Jesus is there, it is good to get a mental image of Him. If you really believe He is there, it is okay to imagine Him standing there. Block out everything, concentrate on Him, and worship Him from your heart. He will show Himself to you. He will give you a mental image inside of His expressions toward you. You may see His face smiling or His arms open to you. You may hear His words of love to you. How loving He is!

We can get so practiced at being aware of God's presence that, as soon as the music starts, we are connecting with Him and directing our praise to Him. The moment we close our eyes we see the Lord, just like the many other times before.

Chapter 4

Dimension

There is a very real place you can go. You can enter, leave, go in-and-out, or stay for hours. It is the place where God reveals Himself. It is a very holy place, the holiest of all places. This is the dimension of the spirit.

It is very difficult to describe to people who have never been there. But those who have been there all agree that it is the most wonderful place. Psalm 91 calls it, "the secret place of the Most High."

I said to my daughter Rachel when she was about six years old, "There is a secret place in the Lord that you haven't found yet. It's amazing!" She asked, "Why haven't I found it?" I replied, "Because you haven't sincerely searched for it. One day you will find it and you'll excitedly tell me all about it."

The spirit realm is not a physical place, but a dimension. Some have even called it the "fourth dimension." I want to talk about it from the Biblical standpoint, because many new-agers have distorted ideas about it. I am clearly speaking of heaven and the realm where we contact Jesus.

> Later, he (Jesus) was asked by the Pharisees when the kingdom of God was coming, and he gave them this reply: "The kingdom of God never comes by watching for it. Men cannot say, 'Look, here it is', or 'there it is', for *the kingdom of God is inside you.*" (Luke 17:20—21 J.B. Phillips; emphasis added)

The Kingdom of God is within you, in your heart, in the spirit realm; and you can only see it with spiritual eyes, not with physical eyes.

> While we do not look at the things which are seen, *but at the things which are not seen.* For the things which are seen are temporary, but the things which are not seen are eternal. (2 Corinthians 4:18 NKJV; emphasis added)

The Lord is invisible as well as everything in the spirit. We can only see Him with our spiritual eyes.

Have you ever heard someone speak dreamily of the day when they will get to see Jesus in Heaven? Like the song "I Can Only Imagine" says, will we dance, kneel, shout or be still? That will be such an amazing moment! But did you know that you can go to Heaven today and every day? There have been countless times that I have gone into the spirit, into the throne room of Heaven, and stood before the Lord Jesus and my Father God.

Many times I have received His love, direction, creative ideas, and all the pleasures at His right hand. The Lord will show us how to enter into the spirit and how easy it is to cross over to that other dimension.

During deep times of worship at church, as I have been enjoying rich fellowship with the Lord, occasionally I will peek open my eyes and look around at the other worshipers. I get such a thrill when I see the great majority of the congregation connected with the Lord and engaged in sweet intercourse with Him. But when I see a few bystanders that seem disconnected—just standing and looking around, or fiddling with their electronic devices—I feel such heartbreak for them.

Some people seem completely oblivious to the spirit world. All they can see is the worship team and the other worshipers. They are completely unaware that there is another world. Because of this, they are missing out on what the Holy Spirit is doing and saying. I wish I could go over to them and unveil the spirit realm to them. Or maybe turn on something like a black light that shows things that are unseen. It is so incredible when you realize there is another dimension as close as a breath or a thought away.

Things Look So Different When We Are in the Spirit

The king of Syria came with horses and chariots along with a large army and surrounded the city where Elisha was staying. When Elisha's servant got up the next morning and saw that they were surrounded by their enemy's great army, he panicked. He asked Elisha, "Oh no! What are we going to do?" "Don't be afraid," Elisha answered. "There are more troops on our side than

on theirs." That servant probably pointed to himself and then to Elisha and counted, "One, two." Then he looked around at the enemy's army which could have numbered thousands. How could it be that their side was more numerous? And then Elisha prayed, "Lord, open his eyes." And the LORD let the servant see that the hill was covered with fiery horses and flaming chariots all around Elisha. It was the Lord's powerful angel army (2 Kings 6:15—17).

Elisha's servant had his natural eyes open and that is why he was panicking. But he needed to be able to see with the eyes of his spirit. It is amazing what you see when you look into the world of the spirit. It looks much different than the natural world.

Some have accused us of not living in the real world. They say that we are sticking our head in the sand. I am not going to stick my head in the sand; I am going to stick my head into the spirit realm. In the spirit realm we are able to see things through God's perspective, which is very different from what it looks like in the "real world." Actually, the spirit realm is the real world.

Enter In

Worship isn't something you attend or watch; it is something you enter into.

You could sit back and watch people worship the Lord. You could analyze the style of music or the ability of the singers and instrumentalists. But when you close your eyes and sing from your heart to Jesus, you change worlds. It's a completely different dimension that you enter.

3D images were once very popular. They are digital artwork with somewhat of a geometrical pattern. At first, the picture only appears to be a scribbled pattern of colors, but when you let your eyes relax and go cross-eyed, a three-dimensional image comes into view. It is mind-blowing how deep the image becomes! It's like you could reach right into it because the perception of depth is so real.

I used to get frustrated with looking at those pictures. I didn't see anything but a blur! After much time staring into the picture and blinking, I finally learned to change the way my eyes were looking at it. Then, to my amazement, the picture popped out. At first, it may be difficult to enter into the spirit; but it is very close and easy to enter. We only need to change the way we are looking and see with the eyes of our spirit.

Those 3D images are only still shots, but in the dimension of the spirit there is life and activity. God expresses Himself to you and reveals His love and comfort to your heart. There is much to see in the spirit realm.

There is a Christian friend in our neighborhood who told us of his first experience with entering into the spirit. He shared with us how a friend of his took him to his home and helped him press into the spirit. It took some concentration and some real persistence, but he finally broke through.

It will eventually become easy to transition out of one realm and into the other. It used to take me a while to get my mind focused and enter into the spirit, but now it only takes a few seconds to enter right in.

Our family lives in the suburbs of Tampa, Florida, with interstates and expansive highways all around. About a year ago, our neighbor recommended a great bicycle trail that winds through swampy woods and around quiet ponds. Some mornings, I hop on my bike and head out of our subdivision. I ride across a 6-lane highway and behind some professional buildings, passing a huge wholesale warehouse club. When I ride down the sidewalk, I come to a little white arbor; and as I ride under the arbor, I enter into a whole new dimension. Suddenly, I am out of the scramble of the city and on a serene, paved path. I drink in the solitude as I cross small boardwalks and notice the water birds slowly wading along the edge of the ponds. The environment makes it so easy to commune with the Lord.

On Sunday mornings, it might take effort to transfer over into the spirit realm, past the foyer full of people greeting you, past the ushers and the announcements, and into that secret place where you commune with the Lord. It may be challenging at first, but with faith and determination, you will find the spirit realm. And after many experiences of entering in, it will become much easier.

The Natural Realm and the Spirit Realm Are Very Near

When you close your eyes and focus your heart on the Lord, you step right over into the spirit. It is simply a matter of where you focus your heart and mind. The spirit realm, like Jesus said, is inside you. That dimension is not far away but very close and easily accessible. It is so close that it is possible to step in and out of that dimension.

When my daughter was very little, I had to go in and out of worship, because I had to keep a constant eye on her. I refused to call my little blessing a "distraction;" so I just modeled worship for her during her younger years and grabbed every little chance I could to focus on the Lord. It takes determination and practice to enter into the spirit, but after awhile it becomes second-nature.

What It Is Like in the Spirit

I have heard many people express moments of being in the spirit; and describe in great detail what they felt, what they heard, or what they saw in the spirit. Often, the Lord will touch me and say encouraging words to me. Many times, He has administered healing to my body. I have seen whole scenarios played out; and then carried out in the natural what I saw in the spirit. Others have seen angels in the spirit, or the cloud of His glory.

John G. Lake, a missionary to South Africa during the late 1800's to early 1900's, had great healing power manifested in his ministry. This is one of his stories, and I love how he describes his experience of being in the spirit.

At a Sunday morning service before public prayer was offered, a member of the congregation arose and requested that those present join in prayer on behalf of his cousin in Wales (7,000 miles across the sea from Johannesburg), that she might be healed. He stated that the woman was violently insane and an inmate of an asylum in Wales. I knelt on the platform to pray and an unusual degree of the spirit of prayer came upon my soul, causing me to pray with fervor and power. The spirit of prayer fell upon the audience at the same time.

The people ordinarily sat in their seats and bowed their heads while prayer was being offered, but on this occasion 100 or more in different parts of the house knelt to pray with me. I was uttering the audible prayer; they were praying in silence.

A great consciousness of the presence of God took possession of me. My spirit rose in a great consciousness of spiritual dominion, and I felt for the moment as if I were anointed by the Spirit of God to cast out demons. *My inner, or spiritual, eyes opened. I could see in the spirit* and observed that there was a shaft of seeming light, accompanied by moving power, coming from many of those who were praying in the audience.

As the prayer continued, these shafts of light from those who were praying increased in number. Each of them reached my own soul, bringing an increasing impulse of spiritual power until I seemed well-nigh overcome by it. While this was going on, I was uttering the words of prayer with great force and conscious spiritual power.

Suddenly, I seemed out of the body and, to my surprise, observed that I was rapidly passing over the city of Kimberley, 300 miles from Johannesburg. I was next conscious of the city of Cape Town on the seacoast, a thousand miles away. My next consciousness was of the Island of St. Helena, where Napoleon had been banished; and then the Cape Verde lighthouse on the coast of Spain.

By this time it seemed as if I were passing through the atmosphere observing everything, but moving with great lightning-like rapidity. I remember the passage along the coast of France, across the Bay of Biscay, into the hills of Wales. I had never been in Wales. It was new country to me; and as I passed swiftly over its hills, I said to myself, These are like the hills of Wyoming along the North Dakota border.

Suddenly, a village appeared. It was nestled in a deep valley among the hills. Next I saw a public building that I recognized instinctively as the asylum. On the door I observed an old-fashioned 16th-century knocker. Its workmanship attracted my attention and this thought flashed through my spirit: That undoubtedly was made by one of the old smiths who manufactured armor.

I was inside the institution without waiting for the doors to open and present at the side of a cot on which lay a woman. Her wrists and ankles were strapped to the sides of the cot. Another strap had been passed over her legs above the knees, and a second across her breasts. These were to hold her down. She was wagging her head and muttering incoherently.

I laid my hands upon her head and, with great intensity, commanded in the name of Jesus Christ, the Son of God, that the demon spirit possessing her be cast out and that she be healed by the power of God. In a moment or two, I observed a change coming over her countenance. It softened and a look of intelligence appeared. Then her eyes opened, and she smiled up in my face. I knew she was healed.

I had no consciousness whatever of my return to South Africa. Instantly, I was aware that I was still kneeling in prayer, and I was conscious of all the surrounding environment of my church and the service.

Three weeks passed. Then my friend, who had presented the prayer request for his cousin, came to me with a letter from one of his relatives, stating that an unusual thing had occurred. Their cousin, who had been confined for seven years in the asylum in Wales, had suddenly become well. They had no explanation to offer. The doctors said it was one of those unaccountable things that sometimes occur. She was perfectly well and had returned home to her friends.

When he closed himself in with the Lord to pray, he slipped right over into the spirit realm. And as soon as he finished praying, he stepped right back into the natural and was aware that he was still kneeling in the church. Not every experience in the spirit is quite so dramatic. You may simply see Jesus' smiling face and feel His love. But every time you connect your heart with the Lord's and enter into the spirit, you will see, hear, or know something you hadn't before. It's absolutely incredible!

Right Where You Are

> My ancestors worshiped on this mountain, but you Jews say Jerusalem is the only place to worship. Jesus said to her: Believe me, the time is coming when you won't worship the Father either on this mountain or in Jerusalem. (John 4:20—21 CEV)

Even today, people argue about where the right place is to worship. Jesus was telling this woman at the well that you no longer need to go to a certain place to worship the Lord. You don't have to be in church. Right where you are can become a place of worship.

You can simply lift your heart to God in *spirit and truth* worship, and right there you have entered into His temple.

Many times and in many places, I have entered into the spirit through *spirit and truth* worship. I change worlds and enter into the dimension that is timeless and unrestricted. Often, I was either alone in my living room or standing in the sanctuary of my church with all the other believers when I have entered into the spirit. But there are not just two portals: one at church and one in your prayer closet. I have also entered into the spirit while driving down the interstate (you definitely had better keep one eye on the road), while walking or biking down a trail, while doing dishes, and in numerous other places. You can enter into the spirit at any time and at any place.

I heard a missionary to Turkey relate a story regarding this. He was trying to renew his visa in order to have his resident permit and be able to continue residing in Turkey. Because of their laws, yearly he would have to exit the country and reenter it to renew his visa. He decided to get there early in order to avoid the crowd; but because there was no organized system and no orderly lines, it soon became a swarm of people. It was extremely frustrating to this missionary because of the mob-like situation. Knowing how *spirit and truth* worship brings the presence of God, he began to worship the Lord. He put his mind on Him and entered into the spirit while standing there. He began to sense the anointing pouring on him like hot oil; and God's peace overcame all the stress that had been rising in him. After he relaxed and entered into peace, there was no problem. Everything worked out easily.

It is so wonderful that we can tap into this anytime, in any place, and in any situation.

How to Enter In

It's simple. Just close your eyes, concentrate on the Lord, and open your heart in pure honesty. Just like looking into those 3D images, be persistent to stay focused completely on Jesus, keeping His face in front of you as you sing to Him. Ignore all the distractions and keep pouring out your heart to Him. If you will do that, I am confident that He will reveal Himself to you.

> And you will seek Me and find Me, when you search for Me with all your heart. (Jeremiah 29:13 NKJV)

It is so much easier to enter the spirit with your eyes closed. You are able to forget about everything around you and concentrate on Jesus. There are certain situations where I cannot keep my eyes closed during worship—either because I am watching my little child or because I am on the worship team. In times like that, I usually keep my eyes mostly closed but peek often. Some people cannot even do that because they have to follow their music. It is possible to enter the spirit with your eyes open but it is not nearly as easy.

Being on the worship team is just as challenging as being in the pews, as far as trying to focus on the Lord. Thinking about the chords, the rhythms, and keeping an eye on the worship leader makes it challenging to enter into the spirit. In the pew, feeling self-conscious, being distracted by other people's involvement or lack of involvement in worship is challenging as well. But with practice and determination, you can enter into the spirit.

Besides just having your eyes closed and concentrating on the Lord, another thing that is helpful to enter into the spirit is using body language. Expressing the words you are singing with hand motions and getting your physical body involved in worship makes the heart connection easier. It seems to me that my mind wanders a lot if I don't put everything into my worship. If the lyrics say, "I lift my hands," I will lift my hands to the Lord. If we are singing, "We fall down, we lay our crowns at the feet of Jesus," it enhances my worship if I kneel down, take a crown off my head, and put it at His feet. It is very easy to do those motions when you are all alone with the Lord; but during a church service you can feel conspicuous. After many years of worshipping at church, I am at the place where I can close my eyes and worship the Lord any way my heart desires without caring what other people think.

So go ahead, throw caution to the wind and cross over. Step over into the spirit realm.

A missionary, Marti Peterson, gave one of the best descriptions of the spirit realm and the blessings received from it:

> "I was in the spirit on the Lord's day." That's my favorite scripture in the whole Bible. I like to be in the spirit on the Lord's Day. I like to be in the spirit on Sunday, Monday, Tuesday, Wednesday, Thursday, Friday, Saturday, and Sunday. Eight days a week. I like to be in the spirit! When I'm in the spirit, I don't have any problems. When

I'm in the spirit, I don't have any aches or pains. When I'm in the spirit, it doesn't matter that I'm 65. I just like being in the spirit. When I'm in the spirit, I can witness without fear. When I'm in the spirit, I can have faith to lay hands on people and prophesy. When I'm in the spirit, I get bold! I get bold and I begin to proclaim things! When we get in the spirit on the Lord's Day, and on any other day, God will reveal Himself to us. I don't know how people can live the Christian life without getting in the spirit.

Chapter 5

Flow

I really love the times of worship I have at home with Jesus! It is difficult for me to decide which I like best—worshipping alone or with a group of Jesus-lovers like myself. It is thrilling when I worship the Lord alone on my piano and He inspires a new song in me! But sometimes, my piano is a distraction and putting on a CD of worship music is just right. I will search through all of my worship CDs and find just the right songs for the moment—one on this CD and some on another CD. Once I get connected and flowing in communion with the Lord, I might put the song on repeat and let it keep the flow going. On other occasions, neither my piano nor worship CDs are fitting; so I just sing a cappella and make up my own songs that flow from my heart spontaneously.

I have had wonderfully satisfying times with the Lord in my living room. Jesus has danced with me, sung in a beautifully resonant voice to me, held me, and spoken many heart-touching and unforgettable words to me. But how does someone find this flow of the Spirit?

Here is an important thought for entering in and connecting with the Lord: look inside your heart and do only what your heart leads you to do. Anything other than that is lifeless. If your heart desires to reverently sing of the majesty of the Lord, for instance, then dancing and celebrating would not be in your heart. And if you try doing something other than what your heart desires, it will feel all wrong and there will be no joy springing from it.

Ask yourself often during worship—*is this really coming from my heart? Am I being sincere, or am I just trying to look impressive?*

There is so much strain and effort when people are trying hard to please God with what they think is the "right thing to do." You can see the strain on their faces sometimes. Their forehead is wrinkled, their singing is very forced. They look very dedicated as they cry out to God vehemently. But the only "right thing to do" is what is inspired inside your heart. When you simply go with the flow of your heart, it will be easy. There will be no strain in it.

I had a voice teacher years ago that taught extremely well. She had a doctorate in vocal training and had tremendous ability in that field. I had had three other voice teachers before her, and with each of them I still felt like it was a lot of work to learn to sing properly. But with this one gifted teacher, I found my voice developing rapidly and I didn't feel any strain at all. She was a Chinese woman, and in her beautiful Chinese accent expressed to me that singing should be "effortless." I learned to relax and to be "effortless" in my singing; and very soon beautiful sounds started coming out of my mouth. I was amazed at the pure quality of the tones. With no effort at all, I was reaching notes in the whistle range.

It seems like the harder you try, the farther from God you get, which is very frustrating. So just relax and let what is in your heart come out.

Let Go of Logic

Entering the spirit requires a willingness to do anything—no matter how crazy, unusual, or unconventional. You will have to leave the mental realm and the physical senses and open your heart wide to the Lord. Let go of your intellect and follow your heart.

I remember a service years ago where the Holy Spirit was stirring us and people were getting into the spirit in joyful praise. It seemed like a pot of water set on the stove that was reaching the boiling point. You knew the Holy Spirit was about to fall on the place any minute. Right then, one of the reserved and highly-esteemed women in the church reached over the pew in front of her and banged on the pew like a drum roll. All of a sudden, the Spirit was unleashed! There was a flood of the Spirit that fell on everyone present and we were so blessed with the presence of God. Who would have thought that banging on a pew would unleash the glory of God? That had never happened before or since. It was the perfect thing to do for that one moment, though it seemed like such a crazy thing to do.

You have to leave the realm of the intellect in order to step into the spirit.

New Testament Worship

There is a big difference between how God's people worshipped in the Old Testament days and how we worship now in the New Testament era. The ability to minister to the Lord out of the flow of your heart is what New Testament worship is all about. Remember what Jesus said,

> But the time is coming--indeed it's here now-- when true worshipers will worship the Father *in spirit and in truth.* The Father is looking for those who will worship Him that way. For God is Spirit, so those who worship Him must worship *in spirit and in truth.* (John 4:23—24 NLT; emphasis added)

Here, Jesus describes true New Testament worship. Just a couple of verses earlier in this passage, Jesus said to the woman at the well,

> "Believe Me, dear woman, the time is coming when it will no longer matter whether you worship the Father on this mountain or in Jerusalem." (John 4:21 NLT)

So worship is no longer a *place* we must go, but a matter of *how* we do it. It must be in *spirit* and in *truth*, from our heart and with complete sincerity.

In the Old Testament, the worshipers had to travel to the Tabernacle or the Temple, and later, to a synagogue. They worshipped God by bringing sacrifices. Their worship was an attempt to offer something to the Lord that would please Him. David, the great psalmist of Israel, worshipped the Lord "with all his might."

> And David danced *before the LORD with all his might*; and David was girded with a linen ephod. (2 Samuel 6:14 KJV; emphasis added)

The Old Testament saints put all their effort into blessing the Lord.

So, what's wrong with that? Isn't that what we are supposed to do?

It is one thing to give it all you've got in expressing your gratitude to the Lord; and to love Him with a great amount of energy, fervor, and effort. But let me show you something much higher: look down into your heart, yield to the Holy Spirit, and let Him inspire worship *in* you. Let Him express Himself *through* you.

> For we are the circumcision, which worship God *in the spirit*. (Philippians 3:3a KJV; emphasis added)

> The true children of God are those who let God's Spirit lead them. (Romans 8:14 Easy-to-Read Version)

The bush Moses saw that was burning but not consumed is a prime example of the way God expresses Himself through us. When a bush burns, the fire feeds on the gases inside of the branches. And after those gases are spent, the bush is reduced to ashes. But when the Lord appeared in the bush, His fire was not using any of the resources of that bush. It was just the venue chosen to express God's presence. And after the Lord left it, the bush was just as moist and as green as it was before. After the Lord uses us, we shouldn't feel exhausted or burned out. His expression through us takes no effort on our part except to cooperate with Him; and it leaves us refreshed and exuberant with life!

The Promptings of the Spirit

My husband and I were teaching on the subject of worship many years ago to our middle-school Sunday school class. When we gave the children a chance to ask questions, one very bright girl asked, "How can God be inspiring us and prompting us to worship Him when He is the One we are worshipping?"

It seemed strange to her, but that is such a great thought—God is inspiring us from the inside of our heart and then receiving the worship of our heart. When we connect with Him, He expresses Himself to us and through us.

We no longer need to put loads of strain and effort into worshipping God. Now, we sing by the inspiration of the Holy Spirit inside us. We flow with Him, and it's effortless. He will prompt you to know which notes to play, how to sing, what to say, etc. When you follow Him, the Holy Spirit empowers you and it is invigorating!

When I play the piano, I not only play unto the Lord; but I often let the Lord play through me. I listen on the inside and follow His lead. Sometimes, as I play in the spirit, I will sense the prompting to change keys, time signatures or rhythms. I will hear little melodies or chord progressions inside and will play them.

In a similar way, we no longer just dance "before the Lord." We dance "in the spirit," under the inspiration and impulses of the Spirit of God.

Maria Woodworth-Etter was an American evangelist during the early 1900's who had many healings and amazing manifestations of the Spirit during her meetings. She said this regarding worship in the spirit—

> "Among the strange acts also that God is performing these last days is dancing and playing on musical instruments in the spirit. These manifestations are not induced by suggestion or by imitation.
>
> These fleshly manifestations cannot be regarded as sinful and certainly not as hypocritical. They are human expressions of feeling toward God under great blessing just as demonstrations at a baseball or football game are the natural human expression of feeling in that lower carnal plane of joy.
>
> But the real dancing under the power of the Spirit is altogether different. It comes without premeditation or choice. It lacks all human direction and control. It does not follow the 2-step

or waltz or any dance ever learned. The steps are controlled and directed by the Holy Spirit.

The whole body is energized by the Spirit. The movements are wonderfully graceful, and often rapid beyond all possibility of imitation. There are none of the attitudes or poses or familiar joining of partners which characterize the ordinary dance."

I agree that "the whole body is energized by the Spirit." It is so exhilarating when the Holy Spirit flows through you! You feel blessed and thrilled throughout your whole being!

In the New Testament way of worship, we no longer just follow suggestions from the outside. Now we receive inspiration from the inside.

This is a higher level of worship. Rather than just singing *to* the Lord, we sing the song *of* the Lord. That is, we listen to what the Spirit is singing, and then sing it out under His inspiration.

Need a Jump?

I understand how it is sometimes when you need someone to help get you started in worship. Maybe you are dry as a bone and have no spiritual energy. Have you ever had trouble with the battery in your car and needed someone to jumpstart your engine? Sometimes, you need the worship leader to jumpstart you, to give you a boost, to stir up the worship that is in your heart, and to get you moving down the road toward the flow of the Spirit.

But, something is wrong with your battery if you need to be jumpstarted every time. We can learn how to look down into our own heart, see what the Spirit is inspiring for the moment, and begin flowing in worship unassisted by others.

Generally, at the onset of ministering to the Lord, you may not sense much inspiration. But after a few minutes, you will begin to sense your heart connecting to the Lord's; and an impression or picture may come to your imagination. When you follow that impulse, another thought may come. As you keep following those promptings, you will sense a liberating flow of the Spirit of God. And if you follow those promptings in a group setting, it will encourage and inspire others to let their heart flow, too. I am not talking about something planned that we routinely follow every time. I am talking about the spontaneity of the spirit. It releases a freedom like nothing else does.

> Now the Lord is the Spirit: and where the Spirit of the Lord is, there the heart is free. (2 Corinthians 3:17 BBE)

I was playing the piano one Sunday during the evening service; and the praise was escalating as we rejoiced in the Lord. I felt the freedom of the Lord coming upon me. So I yielded to a prompting to do a glissando from the very top of the piano all the way down. A glissando is when you run your thumbnail across the keys. As I kept playing, I did several more glissandos. The worship leader turned to me and said, "Every time you do that, I feel so much freedom!"

One of my teachers at Bible school, Patsy Cameneti (-Behrman at the time), related an experience in the spirit. She had come into the Wednesday night service a few minutes late and was tired from a long day's work. Instead of just enduring the service, she decided to get the most out of it since she was already there. So, she started singing with gusto, putting her whole heart into it. The worship team was singing the old chorus, "I'm So Glad Jesus Set Me Free." As she sang purposefully, there began to flow the joy of the Lord to her, and she began to be really glad that Jesus had set her free. As she relished in the joy of the Lord, she saw a picture inside—her running around the church with joy and freedom, getting her friend, and finishing out the lap with her. She immediately thought—*Change channels!* No way did she want to make a fool of herself! But when she pushed that inspired notion down, the flow of God's joy also stopped. The Lord reminded her of something she had told her students that day—"When the Holy Spirit inspires you to do something, you'd better do it!" Her conscience smote her, so she said to the Lord, "If You bring that back up in me, I'll do it..." As she began praising the Lord with her whole heart again, that picture came back up in her. She thought, "If I can just get to the aisle..." As soon as she made that step of faith, the Holy Spirit swept over her, and she ran across the church with great elation and buoyancy. Her friend, seeing her coming for her, was waving her hands, "No!" But it was too late! She grabbed her friend and they finished the lap around the church, charged with the sweet presence of the Holy Spirit. Patsy was finished and went back to her seat, but the friend she had grabbed surprisingly went up to the stage and got a microphone. Then this friend and her husband began to prophesy back-and-forth concerning people's marriages. The Lord did an amazing restoration to many marriages that night.

Always remember: you have complete freedom to follow the Holy Spirit, to yield to Him and to flow with Him. But you should never force anything.

Whenever you feel like you are pushing, just back off; because that is not the Holy Spirit's way of moving. The Spirit gently inspires and we simply yield to Him. Not push, yield.

The more demonstrative your expressions, the more necessary it is that they come from your heart. That means that if you are quietly singing to the Lord, it is not as noticeable whether or not you are doing it from your heart. But if you do something very loud or animated, everyone will be able to tell whether you are in the flesh or in the spirit. If someone in the congregation started shouting or dancing in the spirit, there would usually be one of two responses. If what is done was prompted by the Lord and the person is yielding in obedience to the Spirit, then there will be a surge of the presence of God in the room. But, if what is done is not initiated by the Holy Spirit—but is that person's attempts to make something happen—then there will be a feeling of disdain felt across the whole place. People will have the thought, "Oh, please! Just sit down."

One Sunday evening, our pastor felt led by the Lord to have a "believers' meeting." This is where, instead of a sermon, the believers are free to look in their hearts and follow the inspiration of the Spirit. Several people had already prophesied or sung the song of the Lord. As I was sitting in my pew, I could hear a little melody of notes inside—something like classical music with trills. I decided I had better respond to the Holy Spirit's prompting; so I got up and walked to the piano on the stage and started playing what I heard inside. I usually feel silly or embarrassed when I step out to obey God; but it is better to let my flesh suffer a little and have the presence of God moving in our midst than to shy away. In just a brief moment, the pastor's youngest daughter came up to the front of the church and started to dance in the most beautiful way. She was perfectly choreographed to the music the Spirit had impressed me to play. The sweet presence of the Lord filled the sanctuary.

On the flip-side, there was another time where someone was very much in the flesh. One evening service, we had a guest minister praying for people across the front of the church. A young man came up to the altar area and was trying to 'work up' the Spirit. After a few minutes, he started barking. Yes, he really was barking like a dog. It felt like a wet blanket put on a fire that halted the flow of the Spirit; and everyone was annoyed by it. He caused a huge distraction and had to be taken out by the ushers.

I will say it again—the louder and more animated your expressions, the more imperative that they come from the Spirit of God and not your flesh.

Relax

We do not have to work up something. We do not have to make the Spirit of God manifest Himself. He desires to move in our midst if we will just relax and follow our heart. I used to think that if I played fast songs there was more chance of the moving of the Spirit. I later learned that God's Spirit moves when the right song is chosen—whether fast or slow. The right song at the right moment releases the Spirit of God like a flood. Not what you think is a good song, but what the Holy Spirit is spotlighting. It might take some heart-searching to determine what the perfect song is for the moment; but it makes all the difference when you sing the song inspired by the Spirit.

One Sunday morning, as I was getting ready at the piano for the service to start, the Lord told me—"The more you can relax, the more the Holy Spirit will flow through you." That concept was so opposite of my attempts to work up the Spirit with fast music. After He said this to me, I remained calm and did not allow myself to get into a frenzy in worship. When you are relaxed, it is so much easier to hear the gentle promptings of the Spirit on the inside.

Part of being relaxed is allowing yourself to make mistakes in front of people. We tense up when we are afraid of what people think about us. If we are willing to step out, take a risk, and do what we believe is the prompting of the Lord, most of the time we will be right on. There will be a few times that we may be embarrassed and regret what we did because the Lord was not really in it. But at least our heart was right. Give yourself some grace and some room to grow and develop in the things of the Spirit. We are all growing in the Lord.

Spontaneity

If you take away all the rules and duties, you will find the simple flow of your heart. You do not have to live up to anyone else's expectations. No matter what is in anyone else's heart, determine what is in your own heart and go with that.

Often, there will be many different responses when the Spirit of God moves. Someone might burst out in tears, while another will have a new song bubbling out of them, and yet another will become totally at peace in His presence.

The Holy Spirit is always fresh and exciting, never stale or routine. There is spontaneity about Him, never the same old same old. God is not stoic and indifferent. He has emotions—He grieves (Gen. 6:6), He laughs (Psalm 2:4), He cries (John 11:35), and He rejoices and sings (Zeph. 3:17). Therefore, He likes it when we are expressive to Him. He enjoys when we pour out tears or when we giggle and dance. He likes the whole spectrum of our emotions, just as a father enjoys his children's expressions.

There are so many different expressions of worship. Some of the most common Scriptural expressions are—shouting (Psalm 47:1), lifting hands (Psalm 63:4), singing (Psalm 47:6—7), kneeling (Psalm 95:6), clapping (Psalm 47:1), dancing (Psalm 149:1), and the playing of instruments (Psalm 33:1—3).

But be willing to do anything that He inspires in your heart—even things you have never seen before in worship. There may be times when you are inspired to do something out of the ordinary one time and never do it again. If you are willing to follow the Holy Spirit 'no matter what', you will enjoy the Lord's close presence often. But if you only do what you normally do, what is comfortable, or what the latest trend is in worship, you will not be tapped into your heart where the rivers of living water flow.

A new song releases spontaneity and freshness. That is why the Bible repeatedly says to, "Sing to the Lord a new song." A new song flows freely out of the wellspring of our hearts. We do not have to stick with what we know—although it can be easier. There can be a constant flow of new songs coming out of our heart. The flow of singing new songs is a prophetic flow—just like a word of prophecy that comes forth. I have learned to play the songs I know by the promptings of the Spirit. Then, it is only one more step to yield to the inspiration of new songs. It is the same flow, just a step deeper.

If you have ever seen a little child skipping and singing their made-up songs, you have a picture of the unrestricted joyfulness that is possible. Learn the flow of the Spirit and how to flow with Him. Then relax, look inside your heart and let what is inside come out!

Chapter 6

Power

When you connect your heart to God's heart in true worship, there is a release of His power. He wants us to understand the greatness of His power.

> The eyes of your understanding being enlightened; *that you may know* what is the hope of His calling, what are the riches of the glory of His inheritance in the saints, and *what is the exceeding greatness of His power toward us who believe*, according to the working of His mighty power which He worked in Christ when He raised Him from the dead and seated Him at His right hand in the heavenly places. (Ephesians 1:18—20 NKJV; emphasis added)

In order to understand God's great power in the spirit realm, we can compare it with electricity in this natural realm.

Centuries ago, primitive men would look outside of their cave and be awestruck at the tremendous display of lightning striking the ground and thunder shaking the earth. "Oooh! Wow! That is some awesome, frightening power up there!"

As time went on, pioneers watched out of their covered wagons as lightning crashed all around. It seemed so unpredictable to them in its striking. One day, it would strike over here and over there; but then it wouldn't strike down for a long time. After a while, lightning would strike down again but in other places. There seemed to be no rhyme or reason to its striking.

Some theologians have similarly spoken of God's power as "mysterious." They would say, "You never know what God will do." God would heal someone over here and touch someone over there, but we never knew why or how—and it would be terribly irreverent to dare question Him about it.

But one day, a man by the name of Benjamin Franklin said, "That is some kind of power up there. It strikes down every once in a while; but I wonder if I can get it down on purpose." So, he hung a key on the string of a kite, and got the thrill of his life. He thought to himself, *Aha! What is up there can come down.*

Scientists worked and worked on this discovery and actually established some laws that govern the operation of electricity. There are conductors that allow electricity to flow; and there are resistors that restrict the flow of power. They learned how to wire a house and how to store power in batteries. At this point, we have such an understanding of electricity that we use it in a myriad of productive ways on a daily basis. When we turn on a light switch, we no longer marvel, "Whoa! There's light!" Truthfully, the only time we think about electricity now is if we turn the switch on and the power *doesn't* work. We say, "Hey! What's wrong?"

The operation of God's power should be so well understood that we would be startled if His power *didn't* flow. Instead of remarking, "What a great service we had—someone was healed!" we should be surprised if there is *no* manifestation of His power.

God has established definite laws that manage the operation of His power. If we learn these laws, it will not be a random chance when there is a tremendous outpouring of His anointing. It will not be a surprise when the whole building where you are assembled shakes!

> And when they had prayed, the place where they were assembled together was shaken; and they were all filled with the Holy Spirit, and they spoke the word of God with boldness. (Acts 4:31 NKJV)

There are many laws concerning God's power—such as, the law of faith (Rom. 3:27). Faith draws His power down. Smith Wigglesworth used to say, "There's something about faith that will cause God to leap over a million people to get to one person who has faith." That sounds like a lightning rod in the spirit to me.

There is also the law of the spirit of life in Christ Jesus that makes us free from the law of sin and death (Rom. 8:2)—which means that His life overpowers death. Pride is a resistor of His power and humility a conductor of it. His power can even be stored in cloths like a battery (Acts 19:11—12).

But let me discuss this one particular law: the law of true praise and worship. Laws work every time; and *spirit and truth* worship will unleash the power of God and set it in motion *every time*.

True Worship Releases God's Power

Paul and Silas discovered the power that comes from true praise and worship while they were imprisoned in a Philippian jail.

> But at midnight Paul and Silas were praying and singing hymns to God, and the prisoners were listening to them. Suddenly there was a great earthquake, so that the foundations of the prison were shaken; and immediately all the doors were opened and everyone's chains were loosed. (Acts 16:25—26 NKJV)

As they connected their hearts in *spirit and truth* worship, power was released. Tremendous power! They were completely released from their bonds.

There have been outpourings of God's power during dynamic worship services and His anointing brought deliverance and breakthrough to everyone present. Many times, as the congregation was caught up in true worship, the healing power would be present to heal and deliver many. Evangelists, like Kathryn Kuhlman and Benny Hinn, would spend time in their meetings allowing the people to connect with the Lord in worship—because God's power flows into worshipping hearts. This resulted in countless miracles happening to people without the evangelists praying or even touching them.

There is such a release of power when we connect with God. It is exactly like plugging a cord into an outlet. Once contact is made to the metal prongs, power flows. In electrical terms, it is called, "the law of contact and transmission." In the spirit, whenever we connect with God, His power flows into us.

God's power is always available, but often it is only latent power. The "manifested presence of God" is when His power becomes active and flowing. *Spirit and truth* worship activates God's power to where it can be visibly seen and felt.

Once, I saw a man at the front of the church ready to receive from the minister. When the minister laid his hand on the man's head, the man's feet were knocked up in the air and he fell flat on his back. There was so much power released—and the man was such a good receiver—that a bolt of God's power hit him. I have also heard of blue power arcing from a minister's hand to a person. The minister never even touched the person but got just close enough for the power to jump.

True Worship Releases God's Presence

I remember the first time I experienced God's manifested presence. I was just a teenager and unknowingly stumbled upon this law of true worship that releases God's anointing. I remember that I was lying in my bed one night. My room had been freshly painted so my bed and dressers were all pushed into the center of my room.

In the quiet darkness, I was listening to the local Christian radio station, WCIE, with my Walkman and headphones. The song, "I Exalt Thee," came on the radio; and, with my heart, I sang along to the Lord. As I innocently offered up my gratitude, His presence filled my whole room. That was the first time I recall ushering in His sweet presence.

There was another occasion where I unconsciously brought in God's power through worship. I was a new piano player for the church, and extremely shy. We had a guest speaker one Sunday that was ministering words of prophecy to individuals. This particular minister flowed with the Spirit better when there was a minstrel playing, so he asked me to play the piano while he prophesied. Since I was very nervous, I blocked out everyone else and just focused on the piano and the Lord. After the service, the minister came to me and said, "As I was ministering, I kept feeling wave after wave of power. I looked around to see where it was coming from and it was coming from you." At that time, I had no idea that my true worship would activate the anointing. I was simply hiding in the Lord to relieve my stage fright. However, the connection was made and the power flowed.

There is Holy Spirit movement when we truly worship. The atmosphere can become filled with the presence of God. In His manifested presence, there is healing, deliverance, love, encouragement, prophetic words from God and much more. It is up to us to set the atmosphere where the Holy Spirit is able to move freely.

One time, I was early for an afternoon prayer meeting. Since no one else had arrived yet, I took the opportunity to play the beautiful, white grand piano and to worship the Lord. After about 20 minutes, I was deep into worship and enjoying sweet intercourse with the Lord. I noticed a young lady had arrived and had come up the aisle and onto the stage to join with me in worship. She remarked, "You have created quite the atmosphere here!" This type of atmosphere can truly feel like you are walking into the throne room of God.

How the Bible Describes God's Power

The Bible uses different words when it talks about God's power:

Glory –

> Therefore we are buried with him by baptism into death: that like as Christ was raised up from the dead by the *glory* of the Father, even so we also should walk in newness of life. (Romans 6:4 KJV; emphasis added)

Anointing –

> How God *anointed* Jesus of Nazareth with the Holy Ghost and with power: who went about doing good, and healing all that were oppressed of the devil; for God was with him. (Acts 10:38 KJV; emphasis added)

Light –

> And as he journeyed, he came near Damascus:
> and suddenly there shined round about him a
> *light* from heaven: (Acts 9:3 KJV; emphasis added)

Life –

> In him was *life*; and the *life* was the light of men.
> (John 1:4 KJV; emphasis added)

Virtue –

> And Jesus, immediately knowing in himself that
> *virtue* had gone out of him, turned him about
> in the press, and said, Who touched my clothes?
> (Mark 5:30 KJV; emphasis added)

When we talk about His power, we use many descriptive words.
We may talk about the anointing, the moving of the Spirit, the
manifested presence of God, the glory of God, or the healing
power. All of these are released when we worship *in spirit and in
truth*. It is a law that works *every time*.

When Solomon had finished building the temple in Jerusalem,
there was a dedication service. As the Levites began to praise the
Lord, His presence was heavily manifested, filling the temple. It
was the cloud of God's glory.

> And the Levites who were the singers, all those
> of Asaph and Heman and Jeduthun, with their
> sons and their brethren, stood at the east end of

the altar, clothed in white linen, having cymbals, stringed instruments and harps, and with them one hundred and twenty priests sounding with trumpets--indeed it came to pass, when the trumpeters and singers were as one, to make one sound to be heard in praising and thanking the LORD, and *when they lifted up their voice with the trumpets and cymbals and instruments of music, and praised the LORD*, saying: "For He is good, For His mercy endures forever," *that the house, the house of the LORD, was filled with a cloud, so that the priests could not continue ministering because of the cloud; for the glory of the LORD filled the house of God.* (2 Chronicles 5:12—14 NKJV; emphasis added)

Kenneth E. Hagin talked about seeing the glory cloud. There was one time that, in the middle of his sermon, the glory cloud started rolling in from the back of the sanctuary. Although it was a cloud, it looked like waves of the ocean, about three or four feet high. It covered up the people to where he couldn't see them, and then engulfed him, too. He kept right on preaching—he heard his voice but couldn't distinguish what he was saying. After 17 minutes, the cloud lifted; and since he didn't know what he had been preaching, he told the congregation, "Everyone bow your head, and let's pray."

At another time, during Kenneth Hagin's Healing School, as the worship intensified, he told the congregation, "The glory of God is here. Go ahead and receive your healing. Act on your faith." There was a woman in the service who had undergone an operation on her throat, during which the doctor had accidentally slit her esophagus. Several other operations were performed to try to correct the issue—but of no avail. This woman had a feeding tube down her throat, and, because of the tube-feeding, had lost a lot of weight. When the glory of God came into the room, she obeyed what the Spirit had directed through Kenneth Hagin. She acted on her faith by pulling that feeding tube out of her throat right there in the worship service. After the service, she went across the street to the Monterey House, and ate TWO Mexican dinners! She was completely healed by the powerful glory of God that came in the atmosphere of deep worship.

Plug into God

> Why are you cast down, O my soul? And why are you disquieted within me? Hope in God, for I shall yet praise Him for the help of His countenance. (Psalms 42:5 NKJV)

The Bible tells those who are downcast (restless or troubled) to, "Hope in God." Therefore, being upset and disappointed is an indicator—that you have put your hope in something or someone other than God, and they have failed you. People will disappoint you, but the Lord will never let you down. In electrical terms, we could say, "Take your plug out of everything and everyone else and plug into God." Turn your face to Him, look to Him for your needs, and put your trust in Him. This is the very essence of worship!

We can trust in our God who is fully reliable and trustworthy.

> For the Scriptures tell us that no one who believes
> in Christ will ever be disappointed. (Romans
> 10:11 TLB)

But, we will be disappointed if we put our plug into people and put our confidence in humans—even in good humans, like ministers.

> This is what the LORD says: "*Cursed are those who*
> *put their trust in mere humans, who rely on human*
> *strength and turn their hearts away from the LORD.*
> They are like stunted shrubs in the desert, with no
> hope for the future. They will live in the barren
> wilderness, in an uninhabited salty land. "But
> *blessed are those who trust in the LORD and have*
> *made the LORD their hope and confidence.* They
> are like trees planted along a riverbank, with roots
> that reach deep into the water. Such trees are not
> bothered by the heat or worried by long months
> of drought. Their leaves stay green, and they never
> stop producing fruit. (Jeremiah 17:5—8 NLT;
> emphasis added)

Take your eyes off of people, and don't look to the minister for your needs to be met. Instead, turn your eyes to Jesus, and put your hope in the Lord. Even if a minister is preaching or praying for you—or if a worship leader is leading in worship—look *through* them to the Lord who is using them. It is the Lord who is really ministering to you, even though He is using a person's hands and voice.

Whenever we plug into God with true worship, we are connected to the greatest source of power in the universe; and He will never disappoint us.

The Ultimate Purpose for His Power

There is purpose in the worship service. I so despise the mundane, lifeless "song service"! It is far better to have God's power consistently flowing—both in productive ways that strengthen and uplift His people, and in destructive ways that tear down the heinous activity of the enemy.

What is the ultimate purpose of having God's power? Ultimately, what is this power supposed to produce; and where should it become most productive?

> And he said unto them, Go ye into all the world, and preach the gospel to every creature. (Mark 16:15 KJV)

We need power to fulfill this Great Commission. We need His energy and ability in order to advance the Kingdom; establish Holy Ghost strongholds; and bring salvation, healing, deliverance, and life to people.

> And my speech and my preaching was not with enticing words of man's wisdom, but in demonstration of the Spirit and of power: That your faith should not stand in the wisdom of men, but in the power of God. (1 Corinthians 2:4—5 KJV)

This Great Commission is a divine order from the Lord and it must be carried out divinely. We need power to fulfill this Great Commission because there is supernatural opposition. Unlike Coca-Cola—which has been fairly successful in spreading its product around the globe—the Gospel encounters spiritual resistance. Fish fry dinners, talent shows, and even door-to-door witnessing are not powerful enough to accomplish the job. This demonic opposition must be met with supernatural force.

Your personality might be quiet and unassertive. You might not be a bold evangelist—but you still need God's power. Because, it is not by your might or power—or by how well you can divide the scriptures—that will cause souls to be won. It is by the Spirit of the Lord—and His powerful anointing—that bondages will be broken off of people.

Do you remember those vintage lawn mowers that just had a rotary reel between two wheels? There was no motor, so the only power it had was your own. They look like they could only cut about five blades of grass at a time. There have been some means of evangelism that have similarly taken a lot of effort and yet only produced minimal results.

Now there are huge, tractor-drawn mowers that can clear a field in just a few minutes. Wouldn't it be more productive if we had large crusade teams with powerful worship and praise? They could go into a country—like one of those combine harvesting machines—and bring in hundreds of souls at a time. Reinhard Bonnke's ministry in Africa had a week of meetings that brought in over a million souls to Christ. This is why we need God's power— so that we can effectively bring in this end-time harvest of souls.

> Therefore be patient, brethren, until the coming of the Lord. See how the farmer waits for the precious fruit of the earth, waiting patiently for it until it receives the early and latter rain. (James 5:7 NKJV)

The Lord desires a harvest of souls from every nation and people group. To Him, they are the "precious fruit of the earth." We so longingly desire for Jesus' return; but He is not going to come until He gets what He has so eagerly awaited.

> And they sung a new song, saying, Thou art worthy to take the book, and to open the seals thereof: for thou wast slain, and hast redeemed us to God by thy blood out of every kindred, and tongue, and people, and nation. (Revelation 5:9 KJV)

When His power is in demonstration, we will see the heathen harvested.

> He hath shewed his people the power of his works, that he may give them the heritage of the heathen. (Psalms 111:6 KJV)

Now, here is the scripture that ties this all together—

Let the people praise thee, O God; let all the people praise thee. *THEN* shall the earth yield her increase; and God, even our own God, shall bless us. God shall bless us; and all the ends of the earth shall fear him. (Psalms 67:5—7 KJV; emphasis added)

When all the people praise and worship God with true hearts, His power will be released; and *then* the harvest of souls will be won.

Chapter 7

Group

There are different sizes of electrical cords. The cord for your toaster or coffee-maker is relatively thin; while the cord for your clothes dryer, freezer, or air conditioner is thicker. The power lines that run electricity into your home or business are much bigger. The bigger they are, the more wires are in them; and the more wires in a cord, the greater the capability of conducting more power.

As worshipers, we are like electrical plugs. His power is released to us every time we truly worship and plug into God. So then, we can understand that there is a much greater capacity of God's power when we are in a group worshipping together. It is like having many more wires in a cord. For instance, the potential for a major outpouring of God's anointing and glory would be greater in an auditorium filled with thousands of worshipping believers (provided they are truly worshipping *in spirit and in truth*) than in a small prayer meeting with just a handful of believers. This greater power in the group setting is often referred to as the "corporate anointing."

There is a perfect word for this experience: synergy. Synergy is defined as, "the interaction of two or more agents or forces so that their combined effect is greater than the sum of their individual effects." This is similar to the acronym T.E.A.M.— Together Everyone Accomplishes More. When we gather together to worship Jesus, there is much more power generated. We need this greater power in these last days in order to fulfill the Great Commission and to be ready for the return of the Lord.

Perfect Unity

When we come together to worship, we have one common goal: to honor and magnify Jesus. We may express our worship in unique ways, but our heart's passion is the same. In order to reach this goal, there must be no discord or division. We all have to join together with one heart to experience this greater power.

I played the clarinet in my high school's symphonic band. There were plenty of times when someone in the band was not playing their part well, frustrating the rest of the players. There were a few times when we all put our entire effort into our individual parts and created a superior-rated performance.

Being in one accord is like playing in an orchestra. There is a difference between playing in *unison* and playing in *unity*. Unison is where everyone plays the exact same pitch; but unity is where we play many different sounds that blend together in perfect harmony. The flutes might be playing one thing while the saxophones and trumpets are playing something else. But, when they put their individual parts together, they create a fantastic masterpiece, like the 1812 Overture or Beethoven's Fifth.

The Lord is the one orchestrating the move of the Spirit and the release of His power; and He is the One who set the worship leader in their position. They are endeavoring to follow the leading of the Spirit; but what is in the heart of the worship leader might be different from what is in your heart for the Lord. The worship leader may not do everything the way you'd prefer; nor will they sing all the songs you love. Yet, even if the songs the worship leader has chosen are not to our liking—or fitting with what is in our own heart—we can refuse to be offended or disengaged. We can endeavor to personalize the words and connect our heart with the Lord. When worshipping in a group setting, we have to be willing to give up some of our independence in order to have a mighty outpouring of the Holy Spirit.

All the Wires Connected

Whether we have a good service or not is not all riding on the worship leader or the pastor. We are all wires plugging into God together. How the congregation responds greatly affects what the worship leader is able to do, or how deep they will be able to go in the spirit.

Have you ever seen anything that had a short in the wiring? It is aggravating! It is especially aggravating if it is a light that goes off and on erratically. You think that it will stay on, but then the power is interrupted in the wiring and the light goes off.

Sometimes, there are only a few wires holding the service together. There are 25 people plugged into God, but then it drops down to ten because of a crying baby. The power can short-circuit because of any number of distractions or interruptions.

What if only a few people were focused and connected in worship and everyone else was uninvolved? Imagine how little of the flow of the Spirit there would be. On the other hand, think about how powerful it would be if everyone present was connected. I have been in services where we had close to 90% of the people engaged in true worship; and the result was a powerful demonstration of the Lord's presence.

We need you! Just a few people worshipping will not bring down the power. Instead of being distracted or uninvolved in the worship service, try to participate and truly enter in. We need everyone's participation in order to experience all that the Lord wants to do in the Church. If we will all plug into the Lord in true worship—blocking out every distraction and staying focused on Him—we will see the release of His presence in a mighty way.

Results of Unified Group Worship

> As they ministered to the Lord, and fasted, the
> Holy Ghost said... (Acts 13:2a KJV)

As the believers in the Early Church ministered to the Lord in worship, the Holy Ghost spoke and gave direction for Barnabas' and Saul's ministry. This is the kind of atmosphere where the Holy Spirit moves and speaks—as believers with one heart worship the Lord.

The early believers experienced the tremendous power of this group anointing. In Acts 4:24, "they lifted up their voice to God with one accord." Notice it says "voice," not "voices." They were in complete unity and agreement in their prayer, and it resulted in great power.

> And when they had prayed, the place was shaken where they were assembled together; and they were all filled with the Holy Ghost, and they spake the word of God with boldness. (Acts 4:31 KJV)

I recall times of corporate worship where the power of God fell on all who were present, resulting in a surge of the manifestation of the Holy Spirit.

On one occasion, I was at Kenneth Hagin's Campmeeting in Tulsa, Oklahoma. The glory of the Lord had been building and building for the whole week. When Saturday night arrived, the thousands of believers who had gathered in Tulsa's convention center had become so filled with the Spirit that a deluge of His glory fell on us. I was in the section of seats on the main floor, so I had a great view of the whole auditorium. There was a blue rug between the stage and the first row of chairs that was about ten feet wide and 80 feet long. During the week, many had received personal ministry on that blue rug. But on Saturday night, someone declared that the blue rug was the river of the Holy Ghost and invited others to, "Jump in." I saw with my own eyes a man coming from the top row of the arena. He ran down the steps, leaped over the railing, and landed on his chest on the blue rug—as if he were splashing into a pool of water. It was a wonder he didn't break some ribs because it was bare concrete under that rug.

Then, the Spirit started touching entire sections of the arena one-by-one. All of a sudden, one section of people would jump to their feet and dance like crazy in the Holy Ghost. They got so blessed by the Spirit that they were drunk with holy laughter. After a few minutes, the next section got touched the same way. It went around the whole upper part of the arena, section by section, just like fans doing the "wave" at a football game. This was not directed by any human; it was the Spirit of God moving mightily.

There was another memorable occasion that happened at a Kenneth Hagin meeting in Lakeland, Florida. The church, which seated 1500, was filled to capacity; and my husband and I had found seats in the balcony. The praise and worship was particularly liberating that night. We were very much in one accord, collectively desiring the moving of the Spirit. The Lord began touching individuals; and some responded by dancing in the Holy Ghost. Others ran around the sanctuary in the power of the Spirit. Their Spirit-led activity acted like a catalyst; and a surge of Holy Ghost power hit the whole place. The Holy Spirit blew the lid off of that place!

All of a sudden, everyone in the whole building sprang to their feet and "rejoiced greatly" (Zech. 9:9, 1 Peter 1:6). Everyone was dancing wildly, leaping for joy, and laughing uncontrollably. And then, just as suddenly, everyone stopped at the same time and sat back down in their pews. No one told us to do it and no one told us to stop. It was a divine wonder from heaven, and we were all thrilled by the Spirit.

You might wonder what the purpose is in something like that. For many days afterward, there was a great joy in my heart and the pressures of life felt so minimal. A touch from the Holy Ghost fills you with incredible strength and greater ability to overcome whatever circumstances you are facing.

Stay Connected During Ministry Time

Often, during deep times of worship at our church, the pastor would sense the healing power flowing and the Lord leading him to minister to the sick. But as people would come forward for healing, the rest of the people in the congregation would stop worshipping and just watch the ministry happening at the front of the church. This would cause the healing power to weaken or even stop flowing altogether. In essence, everyone unplugged from the Lord and plugged into the minister—which caused the power to cease flowing. In situations like that, in order to keep the power flowing, we have encouraged everyone to continue worshipping the Lord and not pay attention to the ministry happening up front.

Unimaginable Power

We now understand how true worship and praise brings the power of God on the scene. When there are just a few believers truly worshipping, there is a release of God's presence and glory; and when there are several hundred believers engaged in true worship, there is much greater power. What would happen if the believers in an entire country all worshipped the Lord together at the same time? It is hard to imagine the magnitude of God's holy presence and anointing that would fill the borders.

Group

I have an extreme aspiration to see a global worship moment. What if believers around the globe all lifted their hearts to the Lord at one set moment of time? Of course, we would have to figure out the logistics regarding time zones. Imagine how every demon on the planet would be terrorized and every Christian thrilled when our worship brought a release of God's power and filled the earth with the glory of the Lord as the waters cover the sea! (Hab. 2:14)

Chapter 8

To Worship Leaders

Religion is about God but without God; Christianity is a relationship with God through Jesus.

Therefore, the most important ingredient of our worship service is not the music, the sound and lights, the worship team, or any of the external things. The most important ingredient is God Himself. It is first priority to allow the worshipers to be engaged in their relationship with Him. We should allow the Lord as much liberty as we can give so He can reveal Himself and His power. Without Him, we only have empty, powerless religion.

> Having a form of godliness, but denying the power thereof: from such turn away. (2 Timothy 3:5 KJV)

When the People Aren't Connected

What do you do if the group you are leading doesn't seem to know how to enter in, and they are just standing there looking at you?

This is a good rule of thumb—if they don't know how to worship, teach them; if they don't desire to worship, pray for them. Take them little-step-by-little-step. If you find them more interested one day, try taking them a little deeper or worship a little longer. And when you feel like they're done, wrap it up and try again the next service. People really do want to worship, so we don't have to be pushy or force them. If we give them opportunity and make the atmosphere right for them to connect with the Lord, they usually will do so gladly. I read in a child-rearing book, "Don't *make* your children eat, *let* them eat." We shouldn't make people worship, but let them worship.

I know that sometimes you will just want to grab people by the shoulders and say, "SING!" But since we really shouldn't do that, the Lord will give us patience to work with our group and to look for small increments of improvement.

When my husband and I were starting a church and I was going to be the worship leader, I came to the worship leader of our church for advice. Matti Friedt is a very good worship leader. The reason I can say that of her is because of how often the Holy Spirit was freely moving in our services and how well she taught the people to worship at home.

She gave me this advice—"If you want the people to worship, sing songs with only a few words." That was very helpful to me. When I saw that people were not connecting with the Lord during worship, I would sing a very simple chorus. When they relaxed and closed their eyes—not having to think so hard about the words—their hearts opened up to Jesus in simple, childlike worship.

Another technique to help new worshipers is giving them a truth to rally around. They may feel like they don't have anything to say to the Lord. So it helps for you to jumpstart their worship with a truth. You might say, "Aren't you glad that our Lord is a good God! Has He been good to you? Let's tell Him how thankful we are for all the good things He has done for us."

Quoting a scripture is helpful, too. For example—"The Bible says in Psalm 37:4 that, if we delight in the Lord, He will give us the desires of our heart. Let's delight ourselves in the Lord this morning! Oh Lord, we delight in You! We love You, Jesus!"

When the People Are Connected

As worship leaders, we need to learn how to allow people freedom to enter in without hindering them.

> Woe to you, teachers of the law and Pharisees, you hypocrites! You shut the door of the kingdom of heaven in people's faces. You yourselves do not enter, nor will you let those enter who are trying to. (Matthew 23:13 NIV)

We, as worship leaders, definitely do not want these words of Jesus to apply to us. Instead of it being said that we were in the way of people connecting with Jesus, we want it to be said that we got out of the way and were a big help to them drawing close to Jesus. The greatest compliment a worship leader can receive is, "I forgot that the worship team was up on the stage because I got so caught up with Jesus." That would be affirmation that you are truly leading the people into the presence of God.

Please, get out of the way. People don't want to know how well you can play your instrument or sing; they just want to be with Jesus.

> Now there were certain Greeks among those who came up to worship at the feast. Then they came to Philip, who was from Bethsaida of Galilee, and asked him, saying, *"Sir, we wish to see Jesus."* (John 12:20—21 NKJV; emphasis added)

This is still the desire of believers today: we want to see Jesus. Even though you are very talented, we really didn't come to the service to see you.

My husband and I visited a church one Wednesday night. We arrived a few minutes late, so the worship service was already under way—with lights dimmed, good music, and a welcoming atmosphere. I quickly closed my eyes, focused on the Lord, and entered into worship.

It didn't matter that I was unfamiliar with the songs they were singing. I have often said that a true worshiper can worship to anything. They can worship to two spoons beaten together. They can take any song, even a secular one, alter the words and sing to Jesus; because they are so in love with Him.

After the service, there was food prepared and tables set up at the back of the small sanctuary. Even though we had never been to this church, they urged us to eat with them. There was a young man sitting beside me. As we began conversation, I asked him, "Oh, were you the worship leader tonight?" When he affirmed, I said to him, "Sorry, I didn't pay attention, I had my eyes closed."

That did not offend him at all. In fact, he smiled and was very glad to hear it.

It is not an insult when people don't notice you up on the stage. It is actually a very good compliment when the people are so caught up in worship that they forget about you.

Where Are You Taking Us?

There is a big difference between a music director and a worship leader. We could merely sing songs or we could truly worship.

If you are the leader, do you have a clear understanding of where you are taking everyone? Our number one goal is to take people from this natural world and lead them into the very throne room of God—until they are face-to-face with the Lord. At that point, the Lord will begin ministering to each individual, touching their heart deeply, and giving them perspective and insight into their life difficulties.

Once you've finally gotten everyone into God's presence, let them be there awhile and receive from the Lord. Relax. Don't feel like you have to complete your planned worship set. You might want to keep playing the song that finally got them there. There have been times we stayed on the particular song that was really flowing for ten minutes—or even close to half an hour, occasionally. If the people are in deep worship, be sensitive to not bring their focus back to you too quickly.

Look for songs that are easy to worship with—songs that bring you right into His presence. We want songs that are "worshipable."

(That is a new word I made up.) Before introducing a new song to the worship team to learn, I try it out myself at home to see how "worshipable" it is. Can this song help me to connect with the Lord? Songs may have a good rhythm, nice lyrics, or be popular, but can I worship with them? Worship leaders, it would be wise to take note which songs the people really connect to God with, and use those songs more often.

Progression

Our worship set needs to have a "progression," taking people from where they are to the deepest awareness of God. Instead of just singing your favorite songs, you can purposely line up the songs to step-by-step bring them face-to-face with God.

For instance, you could begin with a rejoicing and celebrating song—one that is fun to sing and stirs up thankfulness for all of God's blessings. From there, you could go further into celebrating the Lord with shouting, clapping, or dancing.

After this time of enthusiastic praise, you could sing what I call a "power song." A "power song" is fervent—declaring His majesty and magnificence, or singing of His greatness and glory. It is grand and exalting and sung with intensity. A good "power song" might be Chris Tomlin's, "Our God is greater, our God is stronger, Lord, You are higher than any other, our God is healer, awesome in power, our God, our God." During a song like this, usually the stragglers begin to get focused on Jesus.

After a "power song," it is now time to get more intimate with the Lord and come into the Holy of Holies. Choose a song that leads people into the throne room of God and brings them face-to-face with Him. Often during this moment, your deep love for the Lord can be expressed. And, of course, He will express His great love to you.

When the worship time has come to this point, the connection is there, and the worshiper is drinking of the Father's sweet love. They have lost all focus of the worship team and are consumed with the Lover of their soul. Relax; don't be in a hurry. Forget the pressure of people or time; and allow the Lord to strengthen and encourage His children. There is no greater place in the entire world than in God's presence, so there should be no rush to move on with the service. It is during this time that souls are yielding to God, healings are happening—both physical and internal—and desperately-needed breakthroughs are transpiring for each individual.

For more information about Beloved International and Dan and Veronica Bean, please visit their website: www.BelovedInternational.US

Printed in the United States
By Bookmasters